The
Museum
—— of ——
Your Life

ANEETA PHILIP

To order additional copies of this book, contact:
Xlibris
UK TFN: 0800 0148620 (Toll Free inside the UK)
UK Local: 02036 956328 (+44 20 3695 6328 from outside the UK)
www.xlibrispublishing.co.uk
Orders@ Xlibrispublishing.co.uk

ISBN: Softcover   978-1-5434-9230-9
         Hardcover   978-1-5434-9231-6
         EBook   978-1-5434-9232-3

Print information available on the last page

Rev. date: 08/11/2020

"Aneeta's book has great imagery, making it very easy for the reader to understand what can sometimes be seen as some complex ideas. I love the practical advice Aneeta gives when you are struggling to find your purpose and giftings in life, as well as sharing stories from her life that has helped her in these areas. This book is a very good tool and I would highly recommend it for anyone looking to achieve more in life and have a greater impact in their world."

- GEORGE LITTLEMORE

HILLSONG GUILFORD YOUTH PASTOR

"I consider The Museum of Your Life an inspired literary work from a wise young soul. The book captured me from the very first page and begun to gently but meaningfully dig deep into my creative mind. Aneeta clearly has a gift which comes through in her words and energy which jump off the page. I would recommend this book to anyone with an ambition to become the best version of themselves in a way that's never been done before."

- JULIAN 'THE ULTRAPRENEUR' HALL

FOUNDER & CEO OF ULTRA EDUCATION C.I.C

Introduction

This book describes the journey of you as the artist, creating a beautiful painting which represents a mission in your life that is aligned to your ultimate purpose. Your painting will be hung in your museum which is symbolic of your life and your legacy. Every chapter in this book, is a stage you encounter when painting your picture to put in the museum of your life. Everyone will leave behind a museum, where there will be paintings of all sizes in there. Some of your goals may have taken a lot of hard work and time to achieve because they were so big, others wouldn't have taken as long to paint. In the end, everyone will see your museum and what is inside of it. They can see the different exhibitions (which are the areas of your life) within the museum including your Mental, Spiritual, Health, Family, Relational, Career and Financial areas.

You have accomplished goals for all aspects of your life so no exhibition in your museum will be empty. It all depends on you, whether you want your paintings to be big, beautiful, and epic and inspire other people to make their own museum just as extravagant as yours or even better.

Writing this book is one of the biggest steps I have taken so far in using my own gifts and passion to try and help other people and encourage them to use their gifts and see what great potential they have to make a positive impact on this world.

Another thing that I really love to do is to be creative and think of different stories and analogies to help others understand what I am trying to portray in a distinct way. In my free time, I love to draw and design new pieces that I think of and can develop. Being creative and imaginative are one of the main things that I have started to identify in myself through the help of my gifts and the time I have spent reflecting on myself.

I have set many goals for myself this year and plan to only get better next year. Every morning, when I wake up, one of the first things I do is pray and think of ways to make the day a positive and productive day. Moreover, I also do some declarations where I say to myself out loud, all the things that I believe and want to believe I am and the things that I want to do in the future as though it is already done.

From the start of this year, my family and I used to meet up every Saturday to look over the weekly goals we all have. We set mini goals for ourselves in line with our bigger goals and check to see if we have all successfully achieved them.

When you start to do those little things at a young age, it will get easier for you as you grow older. This 'young age' depends on what stage of your life you are on.

You will learn more about this as you read this book. I learnt most of the quotes and teachings from reading books and watching many YouTube videos. I give a lot of credit to every person who taught me with their words of wisdom; Zig Ziglar, Tom Ziglar, John C. Maxwell, Jim Rohn and Terri Savelle Foy etc. Enjoy reading the stages to start the rest of your life.

Your Museum

Your museum is your life and your legacy that you leave behind for other people to see, hear and be inspired by. From the moment you find your purpose for your life, your duty is to fill the museum with beautiful paintings. The paintings you created while you were on earth represents a difference you have made in your own life or a service you provided to the world to make it a better place. They are the goals that you have achieved in an area of your life. Once all your paintings are hung, the museum will be open to the public. This is the legacy you leave behind. Your museum will not only make you proud of yourself but also help others learn from you and inspire them to make their museums just as memorable and beautiful.

Sharing important things like this will help many people. You can inspire others to paint the picture they have always wanted to paint but have just been too afraid to pick their brush up.

There are so many ways to help people, but the most effective way is through your gifts and the things you are best at doing. It can be writing a book, or through the music you compose which help people relax or even by developing a new condiment that makes anything taste better so the world can enjoy eating! As long as you are using what you have been given effectively, you can help so many people.

It is similar to what the transfer of electricity inside of a metal object is like. When one particle vibrates, it hits the next particle and transfers the electricity, then it hits another particle until all the particles within the object transfers energy from one end to another. We can spread and touch other people through the burning passion we have within ourselves and make an impact.

You should want to leave a legacy in all areas of your life (each exhibition within your museum represents an area of your life). In the training program, 'Live to Win' Tom Ziglar compares life to a wheel with seven spokes (Like a car wheel with 7 spokes). Each spoke relates to a particular area in your life; Mental, Spiritual, Health, Family, Career, Financial and Social. For the wheel to be able to turn smoothly, you want all the spokes to be of the same length. The longer the spoke, the more fulfilled you are in that area. If you are fit and healthy but not as engaged in your family relationships, the wheel won't roll smoothly because your 'health' spoke is longer than the 'family' spoke. It's important to keep a good balance of all areas and be able to show that in your museum too.

You are like a golden nugget dug from the ground, you may have some dirt on you, some insecurities and fears but, when we face the fire and the hard times, you will eventually be turned to pure gold. Without the pressure, there will be no diamonds. If you know this in advance and if you are intentional on it although it may be bumpy ride, you will feel more accomplished. It's not about how long you live but how you live.

One of my favorite movies I have ever seen is called 'Divergent.' Essentially, it's about a city which has a big fence built around it and the people living inside the city believe that nothing is beyond the fence because everything was destroyed from the war years ago and they were the only survivors. So, to keep the peace and to avoid another war, they make a faction system where you would have to pick which faction you belong in when you are a teenager. The factions are 'dauntless' (the brave warriors), 'amity' (the kind), 'erudite' (the intelligent), 'abnegation' (the selfless) and 'candor' (the honest). Everyone belongs in one faction so before choosing in front of the whole city, you would go for a test to see which faction your personality belongs in. A girl called Tris got inconclusive results because she was 'divergent'. She doesn't just belong in one faction but in all of them. It was extremely rare and if anyone found out, the council would have her killed because they believed she can go against the peace they tried to maintain because she didn't fit in. Eventually, people find out and try to kill her. Long story short, in the final movie of the trilogy, it was revealed that the people living in the city weren't the only survivors, but they were part of an experiment to see if the faction system can keep the peace. It turned out that the 'divergent' people were the special ones. They are the solutions to war because they had a balance of all factions and can adapt to anything.

The point here is that it's good to be different. Being different means that you are unique and not a copy of someone else. You stand out amongst the crowd and help lead and inspire others to be the best they can be. Be a divergent, be a brave warrior, be kind, be intelligent, be selfless and be honest. No one else can emit the same light you can. You have a fire and a passion burning so vigorously on

the inside of you so don't give others the opportunity to extinguish it.

Everything I am going to say in this chapter on finding your gifts, passion and purpose is only a section of the big picture. This is not the whole truth but a fraction of it. You will learn more along the way, but you can never stop learning and gaining more knowledge unless you choose not to.

Always remember, this is the start of the historic museum of your life. Even the little paintings matter just as much as the big ones.

"As for you, be strong and do not give up, for your work will be greatly rewarded." – 2 Chronicles 15:7

Your Gifts

This chapter is about the first stage of your painting, where you identify which medium or what tools you are best at using. This in other words are your gifts, it can be your ability to play and compose music, or your ability to be able to communicate and support other people who are struggling mentally or your ability to teach and explain complex things to others. For me, I like to be creative and express myself visually through art and design.

Wouldn't it be cool if LeBron James, one of the most famous American basketball player was born a professional and needed no practice to be widely recognised and experienced? How about if Leonardo da Vinci just painted the Mona Lisa when he was around ten years old instead of in his fifties? Despite having such amazing and natural talent, they wouldn't have been where they are today without practicing and exercising their gifts from the start.

Everyone has internal gifts, some more than others. Not everyone can recognise what their gifts are as quickly as others but that doesn't mean they are more important or gifted than you. Think of oxygen, it is a gas that is essential to our lives, we know that it's all around us, yet we can't see it. Similarly, if you can't see your gift, it doesn't go to say that it doesn't exist. It always takes time to identify them. Your initial aim should be to recognize and identify your gifts then start to develop them to the best of your abilities so that you can make a difference. Don't discount the small but effective changes you can make! Leaving your gifts dormant won't do any favors for you because you will not be able to see how far they can really take you. My parents and teachers helped me to identify that writing is one of my gifts. That doesn't mean that every short story I wrote was a masterpiece. I would go through many drafts every day until I could move on. I never did it to show anyone, but I did it because I genuinely found joy in writing.

You may already know what your gifts are very early on in life. When I was quite young, I always loved following the arts and crafts shows on TV and I painted a lot. However, there is a misconception that people think if you are living in your giftedness and know exactly what talents you have, it would be easy to make a difference in the world. Even in your giftedness, you must work to develop your gifts. Everything will come with sacrifice of your time whether you like it or not; I also find that I have to push myself a bit but I realise that I should be grateful for these gifts and the calling that God has given me.

Imagine opening your gifts on Christmas day. Before you start opening yours, you look over to see what your siblings got from your parents and suddenly your expectation bar is high because of the amazing gifts they got. You open yours and you can do nothing but plaster a smile on your face and fake your gratitude because of the kind of present you got compared to everyone else. Likewise, our gifts behave very similarly to this. Everyone gets different gifts. But don't waste your time wishing you had someone else's. Everyone has a gift specific and unique to themselves and if you develop them, not only will they help you in finding your purpose, but they will help and inspire others to do the same thing. You may not be good the first time but if you don't get back up, how would you know how far you can go? A toddler, when first learning to walk will fall a lot of the time, but they get up and try again until eventually, they are able to run and jump.

If gifts were easy to find and develop, I am sure there would be more people who are contributing to the development of humanity. It is no secret that it takes a lot of hard work, dedication, reflection and time to become a person of influence which is the reason why people give up finding and developing the gift. For example, research shows that after setting new year's resolutions, around eight percent of people pull through and achieve their goals. Why would this be? Many of us love the reward we get for doing the hard work but is put off by the work itself and would easily want to give up.

Imagine if you are on a deserted island and it is only you, surrounded by the sea and a whole lot of lemons. How would you survive if all you had were the lemons and sea water? Would you just eat the lemons, or would you find another way to make something more, like a lemonade? Whatever you make, you probably won't stick with the solid lemons because you know that you can do something more with it. Likewise, you have a gift and there is no limit to how well you can master it. Therefore, you are expected to make more of it and to use it in many ways rather than keeping them locked and hidden within you.

Even the smallest thing that you may not think as a gift, but you enjoy doing, could be precisely the gift you uniquely have and need to develop. The important thing to remember is to never rule anything out. Every simple gift can become a great skill if you spend time on it now and develop it now while you still have time so that you won't be forced to understand it later.

I have a story for you. It was about a very young boy and he was around 9 years old. His name is Michael. He loved helping his mum out in the kitchen making cupcakes and pastries. Now that he was sixteen years old, he started college and specialized in engineering just because his father wanted him to be an engineer. There was another boy named Peter who also loved cooking and baking from a young age and went into culinary school. Michael went on to be an engineer for a soft drinks company, but he didn't enjoy doing it, whilst Peter ended up being a waiter in a restaurant and had soon worked his way up to head chef for the best hotel in the country. Peter and Michael were no different from one another, however it was what they did with their gifts that determined their future.

It is not only important to be able to develop the gifts you have been given, but you need to treasure and be grateful for them because those are the only set of keys that will help you unlock your door to success and happiness. I was reading about some random facts of the world and came across a story. There was a person who owned a piece of land with his small house built on it in South Africa, but he wanted to get rich so bad and very quickly. So, he spent his lifetime searching for diamonds all over the country but had dismissed looking in his own land. As he was searching for the diamonds, he completely neglected all his land. Inevitably, weeds grew, and it was barely livable. The house was in poor condition and the man also never found a trace of diamonds in his own search. He ended up having to sell the property and went abroad to search for diamonds. He left his wife and kids behind and wrote a note to his family asking them to forgive him.

Years later, another farmer bought that very piece of land and saw it as a good opportunity to grow quality crops. So, he cleaned the house and everything within the land and made it look beautiful so that his family lived there too. This was around the time when many people were coming to South Africa in hopes of finding diamonds to get rich. Few months later, as his children were playing outside in the land, they found a small shiny object that was glistening and looked pretty. So, they grabbed it and brought it to their dad. He thought that it was very cool too, so he set it above the fireplace and every night when the sun started to set, the light would reflect onto the crystal and produce rays of different colours around the room. However, he didn't give any special attention to the rock as he knew that there were many of those throughout his land.

Couple of years went by and they invited some relatives over for dinner. As they were eating, the sun set, and the rays were produced. The relatives asked what caused those colours to appear and the farmer said it was the crystal. One of the relatives picked it up to look at it and he said that he didn't think that it was any ordinary crystal but in fact a diamond. The farmer refused to believe this as he said that the side of the yard was full of them. They went out to the yard to check and confirmed that they were real diamonds.

Instantly, the farm owner became rich. The property became the biggest and wealthiest diamond mine in South Africa. Thinking back to the man who initially owned the property, all the while he owned a diamond mine, yet he went to find his riches elsewhere. Likewise, you have a gift on the inside of you so don't waste your life looking somewhere else for something else when what you have is a diamond.

I know you are wondering how you can discover your gift. Well, the first thing you should do is to really think about what sort of activity you love to do. Ask yourself, "What brings me joy?" Anything can be a gift even if you think that it isn't because you write it off as a natural thing you do but rather it could the very gift that God has gifted you with. It is a good thing to reflect on your likes and dislikes, no one knows you like you know yourself.

Another similar way is to ask other people who have watched you grow up or you spend a lot of time with. They may have noticed something that you do repetitively for years that you never seemed to notice. Use their insight as a little nudge in finding your gift.

Also, try new things, if you find yourself as an outdoor person who loves fitness and active sports, try new things to find what you specifically like about it. You can find and read books about something that intrigues you and see whether you enjoy doing it. If any of the activities you read about or try out for yourself seems to excite you and makes you not want to stop doing, then investigate more into it. This is a useful method for different personalities. If you are creative, you can look into art, design and music. Do you have a lot of opinions and comments on the interior of houses? Do you enjoy music, and do you wish that there was more music in an unpopular style you like? The options will never end. Your gifts are unique and special to you so don't force yourself to do something that you know you don't like just because other people are telling you to do it.

You could find a couple of online programmers, such as 'Myers-Briggs' to also help find out what you like doing depending on the things you do in your free time. Another resource is Gallup foundation, or the book 'Strengths Finder'. Remember to stay true to yourself and be brutally honest to yourself when embarking on finding the gifts inside you. Take it easy, don't stress yourself out and I am sure that you will find it.

Now that you have some idea on how you can find your gifts, it is important to use these gifts and exercise and develop them so that you can help make a difference in this world. Depending on what your gift is, you need to develop that by refining these talents and more will be given to you and not just more talent but new and better opportunities so that you can grow in that area more.

By turning these internal gifts to external results, you can learn more from your experience and from other people's experience. Imagine a fly in a tub with a closed lid, no matter how much it tries to get out of the tub and be free, it will always have a limit to where it can go. However, if you open the lid, the fly has no limit to where it can go and can do wonderful and adventurous things for the rest of its life. Likewise, imagine the fly being your gifts and the tub being yourself. Once you open yourself and materialize the gift you have to the world, it can grow and do amazing and unimaginable things.

You may be wondering why it is important to develop your skills and use them to help others. Well, imagine you having five apples in your hands and I asked for three apples. You would have enough to give three to me. But, if I asked you for seven apples, you wouldn't be able to fulfill my request, instead you would have to get more apples so that you can provide it for me. Similarly, if you have more to offer, you would be able to give and help many people. But you can only give what you have so, by developing your skills, you are multiplying and creating more so that you can reach more people compared to not having developed your talent at all.

Zig Ziglar, one of my favorite speakers, once said, "Help others achieve their dreams and you will achieve yours." If you focus on improving your skills and utilizing them in a beneficial way to help others, you will also gain a lot from the experience. Never spend your time focusing on the useless things in your life that won't be beneficial to you but rather focus on the things that can make an impact. Your greatest weapon is you, so use yourself to rise above what is common and start developing yourself to help others.

Overall, gifts are our precious diamonds within us that no one can and will ever have the power to take away. By identifying them and finding a way to share them with others not only helps you but also inspires others to do the same thing. Whilst adding value to others and helping their lives, you are multiplying the impact you can make on the world by inspiring others to use their gifts as well. Your gifts can help get you far, only if you take the time and effort to develop it to the point when you can say you have mastered it. If you went to the gym once a month, it would be unlikely for you to be in better shape than if you were to go four times a week. I'm sure you have heard how they say it takes ten thousand hours of practice to master a skill. So why not start spending your hours practicing every day on your gifts?

Your Passion

This chapter is finding which surface you want to paint on. This may include a canvas, white paper or black paper. It is important to pick out what you want your painting to be painted on. In other words, what are you using your gifts for? Where do you want to see a change? In what area do you feel most inclined to help or want to see change and improvement? What makes you really upset to see that you have an undeniable desire to change?

Passion, otherwise known as the fuel, that helps us keep moving in life. Passion is the energy produced inside of you that keeps you going. Sometimes it is the energy you have to release so that you can impact the place where you want to see change.

Everyone and everything in this world are continuously changing, even though we can't help it. For example, if I look back to when I was ten years old, not only did I look different, but I thought different things and wanted different things. This therefore means that ultimately, change is inevitable and automatic. Can we say the same thing about progression?

When we progress, we are moving forward, unfortunately, unlike change, progression comes by the intentional acts we do. Passion helps us to progress and helps us cope with other changes going on around and within us. Passion makes us get carried away and forget what time it is. Imagine being swept away into an alternate universe where it is just you and your passion and your gifts. It's a very powerful force and with it you won't believe what amazing things it can help you achieve.

It is important to find the right passion and not what someone else thinks should be your passion because if you don't seem to be loving it or moved by it you will eventually decide to give up and not want to continue. You may have wasted your time on doing something you didn't enjoy. Rather, if you cherish and love what you are doing so much, you are guaranteed to continue to persevere even when things get really hard for you. For example, imagine growing up painting and drawing different landscapes and when you get into the best art school in the country, your parents don't support the idea and instead get you to go to a culinary school. You may be fully aware that cooking is not your strong suit, but you go to culinary school to please your parents. Chances are, you won't be as happy and excited to go compared if you went to an art school. Of course, you would want to make your parents proud, but would you rather do the thing that you have a passion for and be the best at it even if others aren't supportive, or, do something you dislike or does not move you and not give you the greatest joy just to make others around you happy?

If there is something that you really want to do like writing a book or wanting to present a very crazy & risky idea to your boss, or starting a business, but you are sitting there waiting for the perfect time to come along, you will be waiting for a very long time. So, don't wait but just do what you want, what you love, and what you think your heart is pushing you to do, and you will find that overflowing passion within and when you are fully in it, you will automatically release more of that same energy.

Passion is something that can lead you to an extraordinary life. Finding and fueling your passion now is a huge step towards the rest of your abundant future. As Elon Musk said, "Life is too short for long term grudges." I would also add that even the short-term grudges are a waste of time.

There are many ways to find your passion, but the main thing to remember is that you need to have an open mind to finding your passion. If you keep the mentality of not wanting to find it or not believing that it is possible to find, you won't be able to. I know some people tend to say, "I don't really have a specific passion but I am passionate about many different things." I would say that if you list all the things you are passionate about, pick out the top few that you feel the strongest about. "Whether you think you can, or you think you can't, you are right." You can also start to look more in depth on your gifts and past experiences and start listing the main things that you love most about them. Then, look at the common factor that is the main driver as to why you love what you do. Passion exists in the intersection of the multiple things you are curious about or love to do. It may look very confusing and seem mind boggling at first, but if you really set a good amount of time with it to really think, the haze will clear up. When I was about seven years old, my brother and I got a massive Lego box filled with Lego blocks and a manual. We would take the pieces that we needed out to build a house and follow the instructions. At first, I remember it being very confusing because there were little minute pieces which

I had no idea where it would be placed on the house. But, when I stopped rushing and took my time, I eventually made the perfect house. Rather than completely stopping halfway because of how fed up I was getting, I just kept staring and thinking about the instructions until I could move forward. This is just like your journey to finding your passion. It may seem puzzling and look like it's going nowhere but, it will get better and will be worth it.

Moreover, there are other ways such as online quizzes and books that could really help turn your head a little and help find things you never thought of but knew interested you a lot. I would suggest an online program by John Maxwell known as 'Finding Your Purpose'. Passion is about finding what lifts you up. What energizes and makes you want to get up in the morning, and whatever that is, is where you are feeling the most passionate and upbeat. Passion and purpose are very much connected.

It is also important to remember to try new things all the time. Never act as though you are going to choose to be passionate about one thing just because that is all you have ever come across. If you never try new things, you will never know. Be energized and excited to try new things. Waiting for that one thought to tell you what you are passionate about won't work.

Don't let the opinion of others sway you into not trying new things. Even if it doesn't work out, you will know more about yourself and your likes and dislikes.

Many of you would have heard of the famous man who was a huge catalyst in the invention of the electric bulb, Thomas Edison. It was said that once his wife came up to him and told him that he seemed to be over working a lot. She told him he would be better off to take a break and relax from all of his work for the next couple of days and Edison agreed. And, the next morning, his wife was looking for him and found him still working on his inventions. When the wife told him that he promised to relax that day, Edison replied saying that he was relaxing by working on his passion, that is what he loved dearly. He had developed and turned his passion into something so powerful and strong that it wasn't considered as 'work' to him, rather, it was something he wanted and desired to do.

I am not implying that our passion should be the only thing we do for the rest of our lives or it would automatically always refuel itself, rather once we find our passion, we need to grow and keep it burning continuously, like we do when growing a plant, it grows on its own but when we make sure it gets proper sunlight, water and fertilizer, it will grow strong and the roots will be sturdy enough that nothing can remove it.

Your Purpose and Vision

Now, it's time to have a vision. What you want to paint, what goal you are working towards. You need to make sure it is something that you really want to paint, and you know that you can paint. But you need a vision because without that clear vision you don't know where you are in that mission. The wisest man on earth, Solomon, said that without a purpose you will perish. What do you want to paint and why do you want to paint it? When the 'why' is stronger, the 'what' is clearer and the' how' becomes easier. Your purpose and your why are always connected.

I have covered a lot about finding your gifts and developing them from a young age, but why? What good is it to have gifts and a passion for them if we don't know what to do with them and why? Last year, I was listening to a series called "Finding Your Purpose" by Dr. John Maxwell. In the first lesson, he explained that purpose is the most essential thing to every human life. It is the anchor that holds you during a storm. It is the north star that guides you when you and everyone else around you are absolutely confused. I like to think of it as something that is the main influencer or driver of the drastic decisions you make in life. Your values should always be aligned with your purpose.

It is like when you are painting on a massive canvas, which is your life. You have a perfect image of what you want the painting to look like which is your vision. Every single stroke you paint, which represents the decisions you make in life, goes towards creating that ultimate picture. Therefore, everything you do in your life, will contribute to the purpose of your life. In other words, your purpose determines everything you do and how you do it.

Many of the influential people I have listened to have mentioned a specific saying, "There are two of the greatest days in a person's life, the day you were born and the day you discover why." The 'why' being your purpose. When you find your why, you find your way. This gives you direction. When you find your why, you also find your will, which adds discipline. Many people don't realize that there is a reason as to why they were born. Our purpose can drive us to becoming better selves and be extraordinary. Even God our creator, had a purpose when creating the world. If your individual purpose supports the grand purpose of making this world a better place, that is when things in your life start to change. God's grand vision is to build Heaven on Earth. Where did I get this from? For me it is from the word of God itself.

Terri Savelle Foy once mentioned the phrase, "Your calling is calling you." Acknowledging that we were born and put on the earth for a reason is the first step to finding that purpose. Another thing Dr. John Maxwell said was that "everything worthwhile is uphill." We are all going to have to sacrifice something to achieve what we want, so we have to go all out. Only those who dare to fail greatly will achieve greatly. There is a direct connection between your potential, passion and your purpose. Once you find your purpose, things will start to fall into place. Your 'why' will give your life meaning and your passion will help you reach your full potential.

Finding your purpose isn't a one-minute job. It takes some time to really reflect on yourself internally and think about what it is that will give your life meaning. Asking other people of sound value for advice can help but finding more about yourself is something that comes from within you.

There are many ways to help finding your purpose, let me give you few which helped me, and I believe will also help you. It is through your passion and through your giftedness. I learned this from John Maxwell's Online program 'Finding your Purpose.' By using your gifts and passion, you are compounding your purpose.

Questions to ask yourself

1. What do I sing about?
2. What do I cry about?
3. What do I dream about?

The acts of singing, crying and dreaming are very expressive actions and by finding the answer to these questions, you find your purpose and the source of your energy. Think of when Albert Einstein woke up early every morning. He must have been tired when going to sleep late and waking up early. But, at the same time, he must have gotten up with a smile on his face because he was looking forward to another day of prospects into the world of physics. It was his passion. His purpose was to discover new ground-breaking scientific laws to help future innovators. Due to me still being in school, I had to study physics and I know that it didn't make me as happy as doing art, therefore, I know that my passion doesn't lie there. This, however, doesn't mean that I hate physics either. I practiced and studied it as much as I could.

You need to go deep within yourself and think and reflect. Every day for ten to twenty minutes, before I go to sleep, I always plan for the next day in my diary. My dad told me it's important to schedule time to think. Unexpected right? But the thinking time has allowed me to think of ways to add value to others, about what makes me happy and where I imagine and see myself in the future. I am seventeen years old, so consistently reflecting on myself can help me learn more about myself as I grow older. And when I accomplish what I see myself doing in the future, it makes me more fulfilled and find more passion to do the same.

Another thing my dad taught me to do was, at the end of every day, take ten minutes to write down and reflect on the things that I did on the day. I would ask myself if I had achieved my goals for the day and whether I am proud of myself that day. Then, every week, I take an hour to reflect on the week as a whole. Many people may think it is slightly crazy and time consuming, but I have seen changes with how I manage my time and have found more about what I like to do in my free time and what makes me focus better. Everything I had learnt was from highly respectable people who I do trust because their accomplishments are evidence that daily and weekly reflections work.

There are also quizzes and books online which can help you discover your purpose and help you open a new path into finding your purpose. Be aware not to let one quiz define you and tell you how to live your life. Take the insights from it and develop one that supports your values. Sometimes it takes many years to figure it out clearly. It is also said that as we are on our mission, our vision will become clearer. So, I am not quitting my daily reflection time for whatever reason.

It's no good to know the importance of a purpose and what your purpose is but not know how to live it. You need to live intentionally on your purpose. It is not good to just have good intentions. It is called intentional living. The way we live our lives on a day to day basis needs to align to our purpose. Intentionally living on our values will help us align to our purpose. It will help climb any uphill battle which will come your way. Unless you are willing to get on the bumpy ride, it's difficult to reach new and better places. Get comfortable with the uncomfortable journey.

An intentional life is a choice, you need to be deliberate and know what you are doing. You need to be consistent and be doing it every day to make it a healthy habit. You need to be willful and make the choice to do it. I used to think that good intentions were good but, thinking about wanting to help someone is useless. However, if the good intention is put to action, only then it would be a good thing. Similarly, you can think about the purpose of your life, but unless you live it, you won't fulfill it.

There are two ways people live. They either live through their emotions and wish that happiness and the 'full quality of life' comes instantly to them. Or there are people who live by principles and strong values they set for themselves and know that if they want something, they must work hard for it. Your values should always support your purpose. It is like a partnership; without each other they won't be effective to anyone. Seems like a lot of work, right? Even me writing this makes me rethink my daily routine into more depth. But the good news is, the easier and quicker you make the decision to take responsibility and consistently practice the discipline, the greater the compounding effect on your life. Wouldn't you rather put the hard work in and gain so much more than you have ever dreamed of than doing nothing and getting the worst experience in life? My dad always reminds me of something that Jim Rohn mentioned, "the pain of discipline only weighs ounces, but the pain of regret weighs tones." It almost seems like we have no choice but to endure the pain of discipline. But choose now, if you carry on in life hoping that one day you will choose discipline, you will be too late and already be overcome with regret for not choosing all those years ago.

There is a scripture in the Bible that relates to this in Deuteronomy 30. "I am giving you a choice between life and death, therefore choose life."

In the end, you are accountable, your success or failure is ultimately down to you. Leaving a positive legacy will not be as painful as doing nothing and regretting it.

Another part of intentional living is helping other people win and come forward in their lives as well so that we grow together. The difference between a successful person and a successful leader is that a successful person will stop moving backwards and find ways to push through. But a successful leader will help others move forward along with themselves.

Let's not wait for inspiration, rather, be the inspiration. By helping others, you are sharing the importance of having a purpose in life and living it purposefully. Maturity is not just the act or state of full development, it is also the act of seeing beyond just yourself and your needs. Let us make accomplishments from 'me' to 'us' and live our lives on intention according to our purpose.

Your words

This is when you actually pick up your brush and start with thin layers of paint to slowly build up bold colors. Now, you are starting to really believe in the artwork you are painting, and you are excited to see how it will turn out in the end. You already see and know what the outcome would be like in your mind. Your words become your reality in the end. Choose your words wisely and carefully.

Declarations are words that we repeat to ourselves in support of our creators' values. Words create life. The Bible says that "Death and life are in the power of our tongues, those who love it will eat its fruit." When we know our purpose in life and we are passionate about it, out of the abundance of our hearts, our mouths will speak. Words combined with action will fulfil your goals.

There are a few main factors that when compiled together, create a strong declaration and are guaranteed to bring you what you expect. Firstly, you need to make a concise choice of words. They need to be aligned with the will of our Creator for humanity. When you speak in an optimistic sense, your mind is calm and is clear. This is because the thoughts and words you use can impact your emotions of happiness or unhappiness. Next, declarations need clear visualisation. Words alone are not enough; you need to be able to see yourself doing the thing that you are saying you will do. Lastly, you need to do the corresponding action matching your words.

Declarations help build you up internally. By keeping your mind on your purpose and who you want to be, the habits that are formed will change you and get you more focused on your purpose. Therefore, changing who you are in a positive way.

Don't use your words to describe your life as it is but start using your words to change your life. Always speak consistently in the direction you want to go and don't contradict yourself because you can be confused on what you want based on your current feelings. Your words and your thoughts are very powerful. Believe in your heart and confess with your mouth is a formula. It says in the bible, God created the world with His words.

Your words can make you or break you. Your results are a manifestation of your current and previous beliefs and thoughts you had. Your persistent thoughts will materialise as words and your words will manifest as things, so if you don't want them to, don't speak them. They are one of the most important factors that can drive you closer or further from your dream. The more you repeatedly think positive thoughts and say positive words, the more it will shape your life. The more you dwell on them, the more alike you will eventually become. Having a powerful tool literally right under your nose can help make your dreams come to life. These declarations will build the inside man, who has the internal power needed to continue on your purpose.

There was an experiment held in Texas where doctors were experimenting on knee surgeries. So, they assigned patients with one of two procedures. One was the real surgery and the second one was where the doctors just pretended to have done the surgery but really hadn't done anything. They had made incisions on the patients knee so it looked like something was done but the doctors were the only ones that knew the real truth. During the operation, patients were given anaesthesia so that they were completely unaware of what was happening. Two years later, the patients who underwent the pretend surgery reported the same amount of relief as those who received the actual treatment. The brain expected the knee to improve and it did. You will get exactly what you expect.

Don't get the idea of declarations mixed up with magic. Changes may not be seen as soon as you would like, but as long as you persistently believe, say and practice them, the quicker the results will come. Also, don't think that if you say and believe your dreams will come true that you don't need to do any work to achieve them. Think of the inside of a machine with three gears connected inside it.

One gear represents the thoughts you think, another represents the words you speak, and another are the actions you take in alignment with your words and thoughts. If one gear doesn't turn, the other two won't either. Without you doing the work, the words you say and the thoughts you have, won't have an effect. Terri Savelle Foy put it in a good way, "Be your own best cheerleader." Out of all the things that separates the winners from the losers in life, the key thing is that the winners act.

Your Faith

While working on your painting, your goals and your life, it is important to keep faith and persevere and know that what you are making is a masterpiece. Your self-belief that you will achieve your goal with the power of God working within you is a very vital part in your life. Of course, there will be times when you look at your painting and it's only halfway done but you can't help but doubt your skills because of how it is looking. Yet, let your faith in the process guide you to the end.

Faith plays a central and predominant role in the purpose of your life. So, what is faith? Many have talked about faith and used it as a passing comment, "I have full faith that you will pass your final exams!" Whilst that is correct to an extent, we need to rewind a little and explore what faith really is and how to distinguish whether we are rooted in faith or just in the beliefs of the people around us that convince us that their perspective about us is correct. Here the comment means that the commenter believes in your ability to pass the exams. This is a method of motivation, which is good, but I am not talking about others belief in you. Real faith is, in my opinion, a culmination of reading and listening to different perspectives and reading the Bible and having a complete trust in yourself because of the promise you have from God that He will fulfill His promise through you. It is the substance (proof) of the things you are hoping for. Faith is something you work on to the point where what you believe is almost tangible in your mind and as tangible as a physical object. Experts says faith is like a muscle. We have to build the faith muscles on a regular basis by feeding it with our own words. How do you build your faith? By hearing the word of God and by declaring the promises of God. Positive words are the nutrition for the faith muscle. If we don't eat, we won't be able to exercise our physical muscles so if we don't feed ourselves with positive words, our faith muscle also will go weak.

Faith trumps fear and worry and it acts as a shield from pain. It should be deeply rooted within your heart. A faith filled life doesn't necessarily mean you have a pain free life. A faith filled life will guarantee a purpose fulfilled life because it will motivate you to consistently take action.

Moving forward, there is actually a difference between belief and faith. We all have probably used the two words as though they are synonyms, but actually there is a deeper meaning to both that can help us identify the line where they are seen as different. Belief can be seen as something that you claim to believe but have no assurance that it will stay the same forever. Faith will only work when accompanied by action. In the Bible, it says that "Faith without works is dead." Whether you do believe in the Bible and God or not, it is true that faith is not faith without action because then it will be classed as a belief. Faith is such that you are so sure about the result, that you take action. A belief is a concept we form from the world and can change at any point. It has no rooted foundation and can evolve or change depending on who you accompany yourself with. Think about a fallen leaf on a field. When the wind blows, the leaf will move in the direction of the wind. It will move back and forth and twist and turn but it will be in a different place when the wind is gone. Likewise, your belief is the leaf and the society we live in is the wind that morphs your belief. However, faith will always stand, despite the doubts it takes on, it will always be intact, regardless of the views around you. For example, imagine a fully-grown tree with beautiful branches and leaves on it in the middle of a field. It will live through the sunny days but when the wind, the hail, the thunder and lightning and the rain comes, the tree will still stand. Likewise, our faith in God and our Purpose for our life should remain on solid ground and be firm.

As alarming and upsetting as it sounds, you may be betrayed, endure pain or feel disappointed at some point in this journey of life, but it is the risk you should be willing to take. Faith will act as a shield; it is a force which will always work if you learn how to use this tool. When you keep your faith, it will guide you through uncertain times.

There is a reason as to why I am explaining this. To create and to set about achieving the highest and biggest vision possible, there is no point in wanting to start on a painting or achieve a goal if it doesn't stretch you, if it isn't a little bit crazy or something that may seem beyond your reach. One of the true measures of faith is looking at what you desire and want. If it isn't something that will shock others or yourself, your faith isn't big. Keeping faith means relying on not only your gifts and talents and your hard work but also in the promise of our Creator as you work in partnership with Him to achieve something.

"All things are possible to him who believes." -Mark 9:23

There will always be that assurance when you keep faith. When working on your goals, it may take a lot of time, a short amount of time, a lot of persistence but it is guaranteed that whatever you put your faith into and keep working on, it will come to pass. Will Smith, a very well-known American actor, put it very clearly in an interview he had. "Don't start by trying to build the biggest wall that has ever been built. Instead you say, that I am going to lay this brick as perfectly as a brick could ever be laid. It will be the best brick there is in the world. Then do that every day and you will eventually have a wall." It is important to remember that even though you have faith in the project that you are starting or completing, you can't expect it to be done overnight. You first need to have the faith that the small steps or the simple brush strokes are the best there is and you are guaranteed your beautiful painting.

Another very famous woman called Oprah Winfrey had said that the secret to her success was the understanding that there is a power greater than ourselves (I don't know whether she believes in a power or God, I believe in God who is a person and who created us in His own image and who is this power) and in life if we can persevere and not break the connection to the source of this power but rather strengthen and maintain it, anything is possible. Once you make that decision to put your full faith into something and you start to believe it in your heart, you need to speak and act like it has already happened.

One of the many times this has really helped strengthen and deepen my faith in myself and in God was when I applied to a performing arts and design school that would provide and open many opportunities in my life. The year that I had applied had the greatest number of applications in the history of the school and after I had heard that, I was quite anxious initially, but I shook it off and still kept my head focused on my goal of getting into the school. I had full faith that my God-given creative gifts would get me a place in that school. Between the time of my application and the time when we would be told to go for a teamwork test, I repetitively declared every morning and every chance I got that I got into that school. Every time I went out for a run, I kept telling myself it would happen and gradually, I started to really believe it and live every day as though I actually did get into that school. I was called in for a teamwork test and was told that I had gotten through to the interview. I had to send them my portfolio I spent all night on, and I had an interview. Throughout this time, I saw many people applying for the school and many discussions online about how hard it was for them to get to the next stage. Eventually, I got a letter telling me that I got a place. Whilst I know that they tested for my creative abilities, if I hadn't kept the faith that I will get into the school, I wouldn't have had as much confidence as I had during the tests and interviews and I know I wouldn't have worked nearly as hard enough. Declaring got me through the process and I knew that my faith muscle had been exercised and strengthened.

As I am writing this, we as a family are working on a daily declaration challenge for 21 days. I have heard this from a very famous preacher and businessman that this 21-day faith building course is a very effective method to help strengthen your faith and get into the good habit of declaring.

Another method is to use a vision board. After getting introduced to the idea of vision boards from Terri Savelle Foy, I started it too. My dad had purchased foam boards for our family, and I printed many pictures of things that I wanted to achieve in my life. These were both physical objects and other character-building goals I wanted to achieve. I have photoshopped some as well to put my face on some of the pictures. I then put the boards around my room and pinned the pictures onto them. The idea of this is that they are in very obvious and easy to spot places in my room that whenever I pass them, I see them, and I remind myself of what I am working towards. By repetitively seeing this, it strengthens my faith and assures me even more that it will happen. The pictures also help me correct any mistakes I make and gets me back on track. There was an initial worry in my mind about the way people my age would look at me and think of how 'proud' I supposedly am. I kept reminding myself that as long as I wanted to achieve my goals badly enough, I shouldn't care about whether others wanted to associate themselves with me because of how 'big-headed' and 'weird' I looked.

Another method is to develop consistency. This means that you should always practice your faith on a consistent basis, to not stop but keep going because even though it may seem hard to achieve a goal you want to achieve from where you are standing, it will happen as long as you keep persevering. Just like a snowball, you have to keep rolling it to make it bigger and firm and as soon as you leave it alone, it will melt and get smaller. Your faith needs to be continuously practiced because if you stop for a day, you run the risk of not being as faith filled.

I find that another way to exercise your faith muscle is just to take the plunge and to go for it. Like many things in life, faith isn't something that you will be handed on a silver platter. We shouldn't wait for it to come and then take action. Rather, you should start with the amount of faith you have. When you take the action and constantly practice it, constantly see it and constantly say it, it will be developed.

It is similar to how you overcome fear. You need to extinguish your fear and worry by just doing it. I had started swimming at around the age of eight and I had moved into the deep end (around 3.5 meters) by nine years old. I had jumped in the pool a countless number of times and I was able to dive into the part of the pool that was only 2 meters deep, yet when I went to the deep end to do a dive, I was a little scared. I had developed a trust with the deep water because I would swim in it carefree but, diving into it was nerve wracking. Soon, I was told by my coach that it was time to just do it and he had told me that there was nothing to worry about. Once I did it, I felt amazing! Granted the first dive I did wasn't the most graceful, I had taken the plunge and after that I refused to leave the pool until I did at least five dives every lesson. Sometimes, if you simply jump in on purpose, you can develop that faith and keep it working because as soon as you are in it, you feel more encouraged to continue.

Faith is such a key part of our journey in life. Although you can't see it, it will always give you strength and the assurance you need to keep going.

Your Self-Image

Here is where you take a step back from the painting to see what you have created so far. Are you happy with the direction it is going in? Does it look like how you want it to look like? What are your overall opinions on it when looking at the whole picture?

You all have opinions of yourselves, of how you look like, of what your personalities are like and of everything you own. As humans, it is natural for us to always compare ourselves with other people. We always find flaws in ourselves and make ourselves feel insecure about the way we look or act. But what we don't realise is the way that we see ourselves affects everything in our lives. That is why improving your self-image is important because it impacts every area of life even if you don't see it. When looking in the mirror, it is good to compare yourself to a person that may be in the same industry as you and has a great amount of success that you are working to achieve too. It is also important to remember that you are your own person and you shouldn't feel the need to be the second version of someone else when you can do a lot better as your authentic self.

A self-image is the mental picture that you carry inside you. It is the way you see what you look like and the way you think other people sees you as. A poor self-image does not give you confidence to do what you want to do. One of the ways that you can stop yourself from achieving your goals is by convincing yourself that you will never be able to make it. Your self-image can also make you want to stay within your comfort zone and not make you feel spontaneous or ready enough to want to step beyond it. What is put on the inside of you will ultimately reflect externally. If you have a poor self-image, it can be shown through the way you communicate with others or your body language. Ninety-three percent of the way we communicate is through our body language, so our posture, facial expressions and your gestures can reflect your insecurities.

Another way it can show up is through the constant need to brag about yourself. There are people that will always talk about themselves and what they like to do and rarely give a chance for the other person to speak because it makes them feel insecure. Likewise, there are also people who always talk about others and gossip a lot. They put other people down and make fun of others to try and make themselves feel much better. Overall, you can see that we behave in a manner that is related to the way we see ourselves.

So, we know what poor self-image is like and some of the signs to watch out for that shows that you may have a poor self-image, but how can you change that? One way to do that is to embrace compliments that other people give you. When someone tells you how good you look, instead of making them feel bad about giving you the compliment in the first place, embrace it and say thank you for saying those things. Accept what they say and be grateful for it. There is a TED Talk on YouTube that explains the correlation of being happy and being grateful that I found very useful.

Another way is to dress and speak with confidence. Though the classic oversized jumper and tracksuit bottoms combination is very comfortable, you can also put effort into what you wear to make you feel better about yourself and value yourself. Feel proud about the way you look. Likewise, when you speak with confidence, you are communicating in a manner that makes you feel good about yourself. There is a fine difference between being confident and being excessively proud or arrogant.

Something else you can do is to simply stand up straight. It seems very straight forward, and it is. If you think highly of yourself, you will hold yourself up highly as well. You will come across as much brighter and optimistic about yourself. You are not only projecting to others, but you are proving to yourself that you have a healthy self-image and that you are embracing it. There is another TED Talk that looks into the idea of "fake it till you make it" and how making yourself stand in a power pose before you go into an interview will already give you a boost of confidence subconsciously. When you constantly work on things like this, you will eventually see a change in how you see yourself, which will make you want to grow more.

A couple weeks ago, I was on YouTube and came across a video about self-worth. There was a classroom full of teenagers and a teacher standing at the front. He pulled a ten dollar note out of his pocket and asked the class who wanted that $10 bill. As you can imagine, everyone's hands shot straight up. The teacher then took the note and scrunched it up, then opened it up again. While still being crinkled, the teacher asked the students if there was anyone who still wanted the bill. Everyone's hands still flew up. Then the teacher took the same note, put it on the floor and jumped on it a couple times. At this point, the note looked a little dirty and very crumpled. He yet again asked everyone who wanted the note. Though there were some shocked faces in the room, all the students put their hands up.

The teacher told everyone that this is how our self-worth and self-image acts like. You can go through really bad times, when you feel rejected and unwanted and get pushed around so much that you feel you look like a mess. But, just like the note, you will still be worth as much as you were before the bad times. Though the bill looked very unappealing, it was still worth ten dollars and that aspect of it can never be taken away.

No one can take away your worth.

Your Friends

Now, it is time to take pictures of your painting after working on it for a while and sending them to your friends to see what they think about it. Do they like it? They may have some tips on how to improve it. Are they not as encouraging and helpful as you would have liked them to be?

"You need to associate with people that inspire you, people who challenge you to rise higher and people that make you better. Don't waste your valuable time with people that are not adding to your growth. Your destiny is too important." I heard Joel Osteen, one of my favourite preachers saying, 'You are the product of all that surround you in your environment'. This also includes your friends.

Les Brown said that one of the first things you should do to make the coming year the best one yet, is to get rid of all the 'toxic' people in your life. These are the people that always seem to be around your neck, they criticize you and remind you of the mistakes you have made in the past and the many weaknesses you have. In the Bible, it mentions how in the company of wise people you will be wiser. Therefore, it is very important to be cautious of the people you surround yourself with because it will greatly affect you.

You need to ask yourself 'What kind of person am I becoming because of this relationship? Is it helping me emotionally, mentally or spiritually?' If they don't make you stretch yourself and encourage you, they are toxic. Some may even be neutral; in which case you need to be aware of the amount of time you spend with them.

'Birds of a feather flock together.' If you run around with people of no value, you will surely end up like that too. If you are the smartest person out of your friendship group, you are surrounding yourself with the wrong people. I'm sure you have heard the saying, "iron sharpens iron." And "In the company of fools, you will die." You need to be around people with good and strong values, who make you think and stretch to achieve more. You will automatically learn from the people around you whether they are good or bad. They can unknowingly influence you and it isn't always in the good way. If you are always the best, the most successful and the hardest worker out of all your friends, you aren't growing. So, if you aren't growing, you are dying.

This doesn't mean that you can never spend time with them but, as you know that you will be influenced by them, you need to reduce your level of attachment to them by reducing the amount of time you spend with them. Let them see the positive changes in your life so that it will make them want to change too. You need to be strategic enough to influence them but not be influenced by them.

There have been tests done which have proved that you are going to generally be the average of your five closest friends. TD Jakes who is a pastor once said, 'Show me who your friends are, and I will tell you where you are going'. You would rather have one contact on your phone with the person that uplifts, encourages and stretches you than have one hundred contacts of your toxic relationships.

If you spend most of your free time listening to audiobooks of high value and reading books that help you and teach you things that are very important in life, then it is like you are spending time with them and they are influencing your life as well. These great teachers will bring out the best in you. Surround yourself with winners, with people who are excellent in their vocation and will make you raise your bar even higher. You are already a winner as soon as you have taken this decision to choose who your friends are and drop the ones that hinder you no matter how hard it is.

Get around people who want to leave a mark in this world, who want to make a difference and those who are never in their comfort zone because that will become your reality too. Success loves successful company. 'People in your life will either inspire you or drain you.' So, make sure you pick the right ones out carefully. No successful person will be around a dream killer, just dream chasers.

There was an experiment done a while ago, where five monkeys were put in a cage. At the top of the cage, there was a bunch of bananas. So, one monkey climbed up to try and get the banana. As soon as it got to the top, it was sprayed down with cold water. The other four monkeys then tried to climb the tree and get the bananas but all of them were sprayed with water and it happened a few times, every time one of the monkeys tried climbing up the pole to grab the bananas it would be sprayed down with cold shower and as a result, they all lost their desire to climb up and get the bananas. Later, as part of the experiment, one monkey was taken out of the cage and was replaced with a new monkey. The newcomer then tried to get the banana but was pulled down by the other monkeys even before it got sprayed with the cold water. Later, each monkey was taken and replaced with a new monkey until the original five monkeys were fully replaced. All the monkeys that were now in the cage had never been hosed down with water so they didn't know the reason as to why they couldn't get to the bananas, but they didn't even bother trying because the previous monkeys stopped trying as well and just kept pulling them back down. The environment that the new monkeys were in had already programmed them into thinking that there was no point in reaching for the banana because everyone else who tried simply couldn't do it.

Similarly, when one of our friends finds it too hard to achieve their dreams, they tend to bring everyone else down with them just like the monkeys.

Find those people that will never stop encouraging you to move forward, no matter how hard it is rather than pulling you back. If you want a life of success, first make sure you are in the right environment for it.

Your Gratitude

After working on your painting for a long while, you look back and seem to be very happy with the results thus far. You are very grateful that you have the skills to be able to produce such work like this and you are very excited for future projects. You also take the time to compliment yourself to help fuel the fire inside you.

Gratitude is a choice. Happiness is also a choice. There will always be something that makes us want to be unhappy, but gratitude helps us overcome these events. There is no power in sitting around and hoping everything will be alright, but there is magical power in acting and being grateful for what you already have. A grateful heart will always find something to be grateful for.

Three years ago, my dad got me a five-year gratitude journal which has a couple lines on a page for every day to write down what I am grateful for. So, at the end of every day, I would write what I was most grateful for that happened on that specific day. There is most of the time many things I encountered which were not very pleasant, but at the same time there would be at least one thing I was grateful for. We have to condition our minds to find those few and write that down and be thankful for it.

According to research, keeping a journal of gratitude has said to result in better sleep, fewer symptoms of illness and more happiness. Being grateful is one of the greatest success habits of dream achievers. It helps you recognize the blessings that you already have and takes you to where you want to be much quicker. When you start expressing gratitude for the things that you already have, it will make way for the things you want to have.

I was reading about a man who tried the thirty-day gratitude challenge and he described gratitude as the fullness of the heart that focuses on expansion and love rather than limitations and fear. The more you start to appreciate what you have, the more you actually start to see how privileged you are to have things that others don't have such as the place you live, what you eat, the physical and emotional things we have, such as our natural gifts. You will start to really treasure everything that you have and not take it for granted and that will make you happier within.

Scientifically, the act of gratitude has recorded to be beneficial for your physical health and wellbeing. The more positive your outlook on life is, the less you are concerned and focused on yourself and you automatically feel more elated, excited and more active to do more for every area in your life without being selfish.

Another benefit of gratitude is that it will improve your self-esteem. It will make you want to help others more. Your mind drives away from all the negative things that is going on in your life and you start to think about everything that you have been given and that you are fortunate to have. As a result, you feel better about yourself.

The act of being grateful also improves your problem-solving skills. When being grateful, we think back to the amazing things we have already encountered and open our minds to the possibility of finding new solutions and methods to work around the problem.

There is no power in sitting around hoping that the worst parts of your life will suddenly turn around, but there is power in being grateful for the little things you have already achieved and only focusing on them. It won't be easy to always put your mind on anything other than what is going wrong but by taking the time to think about what you already have, the urge to complain about everything around starts to fade.

We all know that when we go after our goals, there will be obstacles that seem so overwhelming that it almost takes you out. It is then that most of us resort to doing the one thing that stops us from getting to our dreams because it is almost second nature for us, we complain. When you complain, you remain where you are. You won't be able to see any progress or solutions to get out of the bad situation you are in. Complaining opens the door for even more things to complain about. You act very vulnerable that even the slightest bit of bad news will get you really mad and anxious.

Being grateful clearly isn't something that we are naturally born with. It is a choice that you need to intentionally make in order to achieve your dreams. By practicing being grateful every day, you form a habit. This will mean that as the days go by, the choice of gratitude will be made easier.

I definitely recommend and encourage you to start a gratitude journal. When writing what you are grateful for down into a book, we are inviting more to be grateful for into our lives.

Your Goals and Reflection

Now that you have finished your painting. You look at it one more time and you compare it to what you first wanted your painting to look like. Is it exactly how you wanted, or even better? This painting is one of the goals you achieved towards your purpose. Some paintings are bigger than others and would have taken more work to achieve yet remember it was all done by one artist.

Setting goals is one of the many crucial things everyone needs to do in order to get closer to your ultimate vision. Small goals are achievable and take you towards your purpose. Your purpose is your ultimate goal and is made up of small goals. Steven Covey said to "begin with the end in mind." In other words, begin knowing what your finished result should look like. Before you even start building a house, you are going to need to think about the internal features and external features and other key things.

You may still be wondering why you have to set tiny goals and not just try and achieve the biggest goal first. Well, if you know the story of Rapunzel, you would know that Rapunzel is a princess who gets locked up in a tower but has the longest hair in the world. Her prince tries to save her but doesn't know how to get to her, so he climbs up her hair to find a way to get her out from the inside. Now, try to imagine if Rapunzel didn't have long hair and the prince magically teleported to the top of the tower. It would be hard to imagine and frankly quite a boring story. Likewise, you have your ultimate goal, just like the prince did to get to Rapunzel but, unless you take mini steps like the prince did as he pulled himself step by step on Rapunzel's hair, there is no other way to the top. Some would also say that it is the actual journey and the little steps you take that give you the most thrill.

Everyone can wish for a way to achieve their dreams in the blink of an eye, but life doesn't work that way, so we need to put in the work ourselves. It doesn't have to be hard if you start early. So, the question we all need to ask, is what is our Rapunzel that seems hard to get and what are the steps we need to take to get to her. Creating goals for yourself shouldn't be a one-time thing but should be a consistent system.

Goals will help you measure your progress from where you were, to where you are to where you will be. These goals will keep you focused. They will open your eyes to many facts which you had never thought or heard of.

Last year, my friends and I went camping. We had a map and a compass and a destination but had no idea how to find and get to camp. So, we made little checkpoints which were locations that if we got to, meant that we were going the right way. Every time we got to a checkpoint, we were all so happy and we felt assured that we were on the right track. Instead of trying to get the destination, we had broken down destinations that helped us. Once we got to the camp, we realized that it wasn't as bad as we all made it out to be. When looking at the big goal, it can sometimes scare and overwhelm us, but if we make small checkpoints, everything is easier to digest.

Everyone's goals are always going to be different to each other as it is unique to them and what they want out of their life. Goals are the red circle in the center of the darts board.

The main thing to remember is to identify what is limiting you from wanting to achieve your goals and find a way to eliminate or deal with it. Knowing what is beneficial for you and what is not shows competence and intelligence. The more confidence you have, the more likely you are to accomplish more and feel like you can do more in life.

When setting a goal, always write it down, "Goals that are not written down are just wishes." When you write down what you want, it confirms it and assures you that it will happen. Write them down as though that is your present situation and in a positive manner. It is almost as though it tricks yourself into thinking that it is actually your current situation.

I am sure you have heard of the setting, 'SMART' goals. The 'S' is for 'specific.' This means that the goal needs to be well thought through and vivid. It needs to give you the sufficient amount of direction you need. When the goal is specific, our mind will provide clear answers on how to get there.

The 'M' stands for 'measurable.' This includes the precise amounts or a measure for your goal so that you know what you expect of yourself. It is a good way to measure your success within a particular time period which can boost your self-confidence.

The 'A' stands for 'attainable.' This means that the goal needs to be achievable. Never take this the wrong way as there will be an urge to set yourself easy goals. This wouldn't be a good idea as it can give you false hope that the minimal amount of work is enough to reach your goals which isn't true. However, don't make goals that are too unrealistic as it can start to erode your confidence a little. By making them a little unrealistic, it will make you work hard for it and it puts some healthy pressure on you.

The 'R' stands for 'relevant.' This means that the goals you set should somehow be tied with your purpose in life. It will develop more focus on your purpose as well if you set the relevant goals.

Lastly, the 'T' stands for 'time-bound.' As said before, a deadline can really help your sense of urgency. You would be keener and more excited to achieving your goals quicker than you imagined.

For example, my goal was to write this book about helping people find their gifts and their purpose and to achieve their goals (Specific) I want to change the lives of one million people through this book (Measurable) This is my first book but won't be my last and I know that I can use the information I have learnt from others to change people's mindsets (Attainable) I am writing this book in alignment to my values and my purpose in life (Relevant) I want to have the book written, edited and published on certain days (Time-bound)

Remember that these tiny goals are very necessary for your ultimate goal. When painting a picture, you wouldn't slap some paint on and say that you are done. You would slowly layer colors on it and would slowly but surely create the ultimate grand picture you wanted. Stay consistent and don't give up, it would soon become a good habit just like a plant if you water it and give care.

Set goals which are meant for different areas of your life. You can have one set for your personal life, one for your health, finances, family relationships and your career (all of your exhibitions). It is important to focus on three major goals and really work on them the most because those will have the most impact on your life. What would be the one thing you wish for right now if you had a wand and could make only one of your goals come true instantly? Whichever that is, it would be the one that makes you the happiest and would have the most importance compared to the others.

The three goals that you decide to make your top priority should be the ones that make you work hard and make you stop waiting around for it to get handed to you on a plate.

So, it is one thing to write all your goals down and start working on them but it's also important to track your progress so that by the end of the deadline, when you see that you have achieved your goals you can also see what you did to get there and your whole journey. There are many ways to track your achievements and many places where you can get more material to help you record everything in systematic way.

One thing that I have been doing since a couple years ago was filling a checklist at the end of every day to see whether I've done the main requirements I have to do to achieve my goals. When all the boxes are being ticked off every day for a month, you can see that you are building a good habit at a consistent basis.

You can also have a different goals book and a planner where you write down the main things you have done that week which are related to your goals. This year I have been using an achievement management system adapted by Darren Hardy where I write out all the goals I want to achieve by the end of the year. Then at the start of every week I write out the small goals I want to achieve by the end of that week which will eventually lead to the achievement of the big goal. We also as a family are accountability partners, this means I know my mum's, my dad's and my brother's goals and they know mine, so when we look back at the end of the month, we are making sure that everything each other did was effective and necessary.

About four years ago my brother and I started working on an A5 book that we divided into ten different areas of our lives, we wrote our goals out for that specific area at the start of every year. It was a good idea because every year we would see how our goals and ourselves where evolving and how our desires were different as we grew older. Those goals books were good to use when reflecting on ourselves. Sure, we did not know clearly what were doing then, but it makes sense now and wisdom says it will make even more sense as we go further. And I am thankful to my Father up in the heaven and my father on earth for teacher and guiding me through it.

There are also many other planners and books from other experts such as Jim Rohn who has a different style for setting goals compared to Darren Hardy for example. There is no right or wrong way in setting your goals. As long as it makes sense to you and you find an effective way that helps you get the job done. Goal setting is an art and the way you write your goals can influence and reflect your attitude towards them. Rather than writing your goals on a piece of paper and putting it to the side, dedicate a book just for your goals and value that book like you value your goals.

Conclusion

In the end, the museum of your life contains a journal of the goals you have achieved and the steps you have taken to create this monument. No one's museums will only consist of happy moments and huge successes. John Maxwell reminds us to fail forward. Every setback you may have only adds to your paintings. It makes the painting more realistic to have mistakes on it. More than how the museum looks like from the outside, it's about the true master pieces of art that is inside that defines the museum.

Make your museum worthwhile and have it filled with achievements that you never even thought were possible.

"Commit to the Lord whatever you do, and your plans will succeed."

Printed in the United States
By Bookmasters